Practical Pre-School Books

PLANNING FOR THE EARLY YEARS

Series editor Jennie Lindon

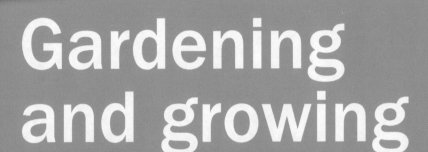

Gardening and growing

How to plan learning opportunities that **engage** and **interest** children

By Alistair Bryce-Clegg

BIRTH TO FIVE

Contents

Published by Practical Pre-School Books, A Division of MA Education Ltd, St Jude's Church, Dulwich Road, Herne Hill, London, SE24 0PB.

Tel: 020 7738 5454 www.practicalpreschoolbooks.com

© MA Education Ltd 2012

Series design: Alison Cutler **fonthill**creative 01722 717043

Series editor: Jennie Lindon

All images © MA Education Ltd, other than the images listed below.
All photos other than the below taken by Lucie Carlier.
Front cover image © iStockphoto.com/Cameron Whitman.
Pages 20, 23, 28 and 31 taken by Fiona Bryce-Clegg.

Author's acknowledgements:

...n and staff at the Hamstel Infant and ...or participating in the photographs.

Planning to make a difference for children

A child-friendly approach to planning

Young children benefit from reflective adults who plan ahead on the basis of knowing those children: their current interests and abilities, but also what they are keen to puzzle out and learn. Each title in this series of 'Planning for the Early Years' offers a specific focus for children's learning, with activities for you to fine-tune for young girls and boys whom you know well. These adult-initiated activities happen within a day or session when children have plenty of time for initiating and organising their own play. Your focus for the activities is short term; plan ahead just enough so that everything is poised to go.

Thoughtful planning ensures that children enjoy a variety of interesting experiences that will stretch their physical skills, social and communicative abilities and their knowledge of their own world. A flair for creative expression should be nurtured in early childhood. The national frameworks recognise that creativity is about encouraging open-ended thinking and problem-solving, just as much as opportunities for children to enjoy making something tangible. Plans that make a difference for young children connect closely with their current ability and understanding, yet offer a comfortable stretch beyond what is currently easy.

Adult-initiated activities build on children's current interests. However, they are also planned because familiar adults have good reasons to expect that this experience will engage the children. Young children cannot ask to do something again, or develop their own version, until they have that first-time experience. The best plans are flexible; there is scope for the children to influence the details and adults can respond to what actually happens.

Planning is a process that involves thinking, discussing, doing and reflecting. Young children become part of this process, showing you their interests and preferences by their actions just as much as their words, when spoken language develops. Adult planning energy will have created an accessible, well-resourced learning environment – indoors and outdoors. The suggested activities in this book happen against that backdrop and children's new interests can be met by enhancements to the environment – changes that they can help to organise.

Why explore gardening and growing with young children?

Planting a seed and watching it grow can be a truly magical experience for young children. It can give them a real sense of awe and wonder – as well as developing the skills of nurture and patience!

There is no better way to learn anything than through your own first-hand experience. You cannot teach someone how mud feels when you squelch it between your fingers, how it feels to have ice-cold rain trickle down the back of your coat or how the air smells different as the seasons change. These things have to be experienced first hand and the more opportunities children get to work and play outdoors the more opportunities they will have to learn.

A trip to the park, the local woods or the garden centre will all help to build children's knowledge and understanding of the many varieties of growing things that exist and how and where they grow. As valuable as they are, these trips are 'events' and usually only happen occasionally. For real impact children need to be able to see the beginning, middle and end of the growing process. They need to see how the seed they have planted begins to shoot, know it was because of their nurture that the plant continued to grow and feel the immense pleasure of having been the 'creator' of a little piece of garden magic.

The great thing about gardening and growing is that all of this learning can take place in the smallest of spaces. With just a few resources, some basic knowledge and a lot of enthusiasm, you can create limitless opportunities for learning.

One of the most fascinating things about the outdoors for children is that no two days are ever the same. The seasons and the weather ensure that there is always something different to look at, touch, taste or smell.

Thoughtful adults: effective planning

The planning process starts with what it is that you want the children to learn about gardening and growing. For babies and very young children, being outside offers them a whole new range of smells, sounds, things to see, touch and taste. If you are working with very young children or children who have very limited experience of outdoors, then you would want to build up their confidence and familiarity with being in an outside space and using all of their senses to explore and enjoy it.

As children get older and more experienced, then you would be planning to increase their understanding of how 'growing' works, not necessarily in the most technical of terms, but how a flower becomes a flower and a bean becomes a bean. Simply, where does it start, what does it need to survive and where does it end. Do all plants carry on growing for ever? Why do some plants produce seeds at the end of the summer? Why do the leaves fall off the trees in autumn? These are questions that children will need help to find the answers to. Think about what you know happens to plants and flowers, how nature changes in response to the seasons and the weather. Most importantly, think ahead! If you anticipate what is about to change in your outdoor space then you can plan activities that help children to explore possibilities for why things are happening. If a child finds the solution to their questions from their own discovery it is far more powerful than if they were just told the outcome by an adult. The role of a thoughtful adult is to anticipate possible questions and then plan activities to guide the child to discovering the answer.

The developmental learning journey

Any outdoor space, however small, can offer huge opportunities for learning for children of all ages and across the whole span of their development. For babies, the journey starts with sensing something different. The feeling of the wind against your skin, the different smells of the outdoors and also the feeling of sitting or lying on grass, moss or paving stone! Even in a small space, have you planted things like bamboo or grasses that will make a rustling sound in the wind and be soft to a babies' touch? Have you planted pots of herbs that when rubbed onto skin or fabric, will give your baby something new to smell (and touch)?

As children begin to develop and grow, their first love in the garden is usually to dig. Knowing this to be true, it is often useful to designate a digging space away from where you have just planted those first precious seeds.

Children at this stage will begin to show real interest in the world around them on a large scale – changes in seasons, effects of the weather, summer flowers and autumn leaves. They will also become inquisitive on a smaller scale, enjoying the opportunity to look at plants and their growth close up. This is when children often begin to make the link between food that they eat and the fact that it is grown. They may be very used to seeing strawberries in the fridge but do they realise those strawberries came from a plant?

Once the concept of growing becomes more familiar to children, the next step in their development is to understand more about how plants grow, how a seed can become a plant and what conditions it needs to thrive.

The personal learning journey

There are many aspects of gardening and growing that are relevant to all children. The key to effective learning is understanding that different children have different life and learning experiences and therefore need different input at different stages of their development.

When you are considering what to plan for the children that you work with, it is key to think of them not by the age, but by their stage of development in the area you are going to teach. Not all two-year-olds will have had the opportunity to play out in a big garden space, dig in the soil, listen for birds and plant their own vegetables – but some will. Therefore it is really important that you try and gain as much knowledge of a child's prior leaning as possible before you start.

A subject like gardening and growing can be used really easily to help build and strengthen good home/ setting links because you can grow a seed easily and cheaply almost anywhere. This subject provides lots of opportunities for joint projects and can also prove successful in encouraging other members of the children's family to come and work alongside you in your setting. This might involve helping you to cultivate and maintain your growing space but it could also be to come and help you to 'make' using the produce you have harvested.

Once you have established what your children know about the outdoor environment, you can then plan activities to take their learning forward. As with any

planning, engagement is the key. If the children are not engaged then they will not learn. The more you can make the planning process personal to their individual needs and preferences then the more success you will have with the outcomes.

Children make a difference to adult plans

Our role as key adults in children's learning process is to ensure that we plan an environment and activity which supports giving children the opportunity to explore an idea. As adults we must not 'tell' the answers, but guide and encourage a child along their journey of discovery until eventually they reach the correct conclusion.

Learning that takes place like this is powerful. It is based around children's immediate interests and gives both the child and the adult the opportunity to spend quality time talking, thinking and learning together.

A planning process that really encourages children to discover for themselves has to be flexible. Every time you plan an activity on paper you only plan one possible outcome. When you then introduce your activity idea to children you should be prepared for the very distinct possibility that they will do something else with it!

Children will often change the direction of your planning because there is something else happening that is of more interest to them. During your planning process, think about the children you are planning for as individuals and what you know really interests them at the moment.

Even if you think of a great idea for an activity, ask yourself if your children will be genuinely interested in it. If the answer is 'no' then this is one to save for another time.

Experiences worth talking and thinking about

Not all children will respond to the same activity in the same way. Children are constantly trying to put their theories to the test by hands-on doing and exploring. The presence of the adult in these situations is to help and guide that process, not tell the children what they have to do next. If you only have 15 minutes to carry out your planned activity before the next group of children come along, then this is never going to happen!

It is sometimes hard to find the balance between talking and listening for adults. We often feel obliged to 'teach' all of the time and that usually involves filling any gaps with adult talk. As I have said previously, quality learning and teaching comes from children having periods of time to explore, experience, think and return to a task to apply what they have learnt!

Our role as adults is to help the learning process along; sometimes with direct teaching and sometimes with careful watching and listening. Most children love to talk and are keen to share what they are thinking. Children very quickly work out which adults listen to them and which do not.

It is important to keep an open mind when working on any activity with children. Have a goal but don't discount the possibility that thing could well change.

Through careful listening to children's talk during their learning and play we can make really valuable assessments of their understanding of the world around them and what they are really interested in.

For instance, I once observed two children having a long discussion about the fact that bees lived inside flowers. They had thought this because they had seen them flying in and out collecting pollen. This led to lots of practical activities around finding out about bees.

Scope for creativity

Creativity is not just about art, dance and drama. It is a way of thinking. Young children need to be given lots of opportunities to develop the ability to think creatively.

We want to encourage them to look for answers and not just wait to be told – to try and come up with multiple ways to solve a problem and not just give up after the first thing they try doesn't work. Children also need to learn that it can be good, even exciting, to take a risk. It is worth remembering that risk isn't always physical, it can also be intellectual.

To be able to think creatively, babies and children need lots of different experiences to draw on. They need to have had lots of time to try different things in a variety of different ways. To be able to do this, children need to be able to lead their own learning and have the opportunity to interpret the world around them in their own unique way.

Our role as adults is to create an environment that actively encourages children to 'think' and 'make' in a creative way. We need to provide a good mix of adult-directed 'taught' activities and time for children to discover and explore. We need to make time to quietly observe the children at play and actively listen to their interactions with us and others. These observations will show us what the children already know and how they think. This knowledge will then shape how we plan our environment, activities and enhancements.

Our ultimate aim is to inspire children to want to know more, to be eager to learn and be engaged in the opportunities that we create for them and, just as importantly, the ones we let them create for themselves.

UK frameworks and planning

Early childhood starts with babies and stretches to five or six years of age. Within the four nations of the UK, England is the only country to have moved to a Birth to Five years framework. Northern Ireland and Scotland have two documents to cover the early years span; Wales currently has a single document. (See page 32 for references.)

However, similar principles within national documents emphasise that:

- Practitioners need to take a personalised approach, supported by flexible planning that takes full account of the current abilities of individual babies and children, as well as likely next steps.

- Young children learn best when there is plenty of scope for child-initiated activities, within a learning environment well resourced for play and friendly conversation.

- Adult-initiated activities should enable children to be mentally and physically active within those experiences and children's interests influence the development of adult plans.

- Headings for aspects of development vary, but the consistent message is that child development is holistic. The areas of learning are presented separately to ensure that nothing is overlooked. Yet, day by day, young children, absorbed in an engaging activity, will learn in ways that combine several different areas.

- Children's secure learning depends on practitioners who value, nurture and foster close relationships with children and their family.

Early years practitioners need to be very familiar with their relevant national framework, including the way in which areas of development are organised. Different phrases are used to refer to aspects of children's learning. Yet, there is a consistent emphasis on the central importance of young children's personal, social and emotional development and on building a secure base of communication and spoken language. Along with active respect for children's physical development and wellbeing, these areas of development are the crucial foundations for other areas of young learning.

Wherever early years practitioners live and work, they need to grasp how young children make sense of the early mathematical concepts and how they extend their general knowledge of the wider world. A flair for creative expression should be nurtured in early childhood and the national frameworks acknowledge that creativity is as much about how children think as the pleasure in making something tangible.

The approach to planning, in each national framework, links the key components of:

- **Alert observation** by practitioners who come to know individual children very well. Observation is a combination of spontaneously noticing what children do and a more planned watching and listening.

- **Assessment** – a process of making sense – of what has been observed, so that understanding can inform what is offered to individual children and small groups in the immediate and relatively near future.

- **Short-term planning** shown in adult actions to add resources, so that children can extend their observed interests. Equally short-term, flexible planning for adult-initiated (and maybe adult-led) activities that are likely to engage children and stretch their current abilities or knowledge.

This continual approach is sometimes described as a 'planning cycle', because it is ongoing. Observation, assessment and planning are not separate practitioner activities, each in their own little box. Adult thoughtfulness can be provoked at any point: by what you observe, what you have learned by bringing together your knowledge of this child, and by events within spontaneous play and conversation, or slightly more organised activities. Finally, national early years frameworks raise the importance of children being involved in the process of planning, appropriately for their age. Young children need to be confident that their views and preferences, however expressed, make a difference to what happens day by day.

Making connections with home life

When children feel at ease in their immediate surroundings, their potential for engagement and therefore learning, significantly increases. The more links that we can make between aspects of our setting and a child's home life the more secure they will feel.

Of course we cannot make our setting environments a carbon copy of every child's home environment – this would be impractical and impossible as the children that we work with will come from very different and often very diverse social and cultural backgrounds.

What we ideally want to do is to incorporate 'aspects' or 'flavours' of home life that are familiar to the children. By having open and regular communication with other significant family members the child will see that there are strong connections between your setting and the place that they know as 'home'.

The more a child's family understands about what sort of activities you are planning at your setting and why, the more opportunities they have to get involved and support you in a learning partnership.

With any activity where children are going to be going outside into a very free and often alien environment, there is the potential for their families to become concerned about the children's welfare.

In todays society children 'play out' on their own less than ever before. Partly because adults are often concerned about their safety but also because there is a huge amount of technology that is readily available to children, which encourages them to sit inside to watch or play.

Playing and learning outdoors often involves getting dirty and I have had many conversations with parents who have asked if their children can be exempt from outdoor play because they don't want them to get wet or dirty especially when they have come to your setting in their designer clothing!

Although we should be sympathetic to the wishes of parents and guardians we also have a duty to provide the best educational experiences that we can for the children in our care. Our commitment to the value of good (messy) outdoor play may require us to give lots of information for parents and guardians. Regular conversations at the setting door, displays that show the value of outdoor play and the learning that has been achieved, letters home and parent's meetings will all help to ensure that this message is being heard and understood.

Finding out from adults what sort of outdoor space is available to the children at home will help you to assess their existing knowledge and need. Some children will have no access to an outdoor space other than your setting. Others may have had experience of a wide range of outdoor features. The more information you can gather about their experiences the better.

By asking other adults within a child's family to come in and work with you and their child, you are not only strengthening the relationship between home and setting, but also creating another opportunity to find out about children's individual and personal preferences.

As with most early years activities, the motto for outdoors is 'be prepared'. If you want to offer a range of experiences to children in a range of weather conditions then you are going to need to do some planning in advance. If you don't want your children to get soaked in the rain then make sure you have waterproof clothing and wellingtons available. It is worth bearing in mind that a lot of children will never have had to put on a pair of waterproof trousers before – so make sure you practise before the first outing!

For children who have had little or no experience of being outdoors in a natural environment the whole experience can be a little overwhelming. If you know that this is the case then slowly introduce that child to your outdoor space and try and do it through activities that you know they enjoy and use resources that they are familiar with.

Because so much of the learning that we do in our outdoor spaces involves our senses, there are lots of activities that you can send home with children for them to do alongside their adults. How many different bird songs can you hear out of your window? How many different coloured autumn leaves can you collect? Can you touch five smooth things and five spikey things and bring them in for us all to have a look at?

Often, the simpler the idea, the better. Try and make it fun and not feel like worksheet 'homework'. You don't just want the children (and adults) to learn about outdoors, you also want the whole family to appreciate the relevance and importance of how you are teaching in the Early Years Foundation Stage and how high-level engagement, and often a bit of mess, really helps children to learn.

Learning about garden treasures

Great learning occurs when children are given lots of time and repeated opportunities to find out things for themselves. For a very young child to truly understand a concept, their brain has had to go through a number of processes of evaluating and re-evaluating what they are discovering. The development of young children's brains can be enhanced with opportunities for them to practise skills and revisit experiences that engage them.

What do you need to do beforehand?

If you were planning to do this activity with babies and very young children then you would first collect the items that you want them to experience. Think about why you are choosing each one. Is it for size, shape, texture, colour, smell or taste?

Because it is one of the most sensitive parts of the developing body, babies and young children often put objects they wish to experience into their mouths. For this reason it is essential that you have carried out an appropriate risk assessment for this activity. For example, put scented herbs in small muslin bags that make them easier to handle and harder to eat.

If the children are older, encourage them to collect their own objects. A clear bag or bucket is always a good idea so that they (and you) can see what they have collected as they go along.

Good exploration needs time and space and somewhere appropriate to store any items for activities revisited.

Ideally this activity should take place outside but if you are indoors, ensure there is enough space for the children to explore what they have got and enough items for each child.

Children have an innate sense of curiosity that inspires them to explore and investigate the world around them. They are pre-programmed to look, touch and feel what is around them and within reach. It is important that we don't restrict their explorations to indoor activities only and that we allow them equal opportunity to explore their outdoor environment. If you are working with babies who are not mobile enough to explore on their own, then you can bring the outdoors to them though heuristic baskets.

Heuristic means 'helping to find out or discover by trial and error'. It comes from the same source as the word 'eureka', which means 'I found it'. We can enhance babies sensory experiences by creating a collection of things to discover and explore taken from the outdoors. This type of learning experience is typified by the work of Elinor Goldschmied and Anita Hughes ('Heuristic Play with Objects' (1992) National Children's Bureau) with their 'treasure basket' experiences.

An opportunity to learn about garden treasures

This is an activity that should be repeated regularly to allow children to really explore and become familiar with what is around them.

The focus of the activity will change depending on the age of the child, their experience of outdoor spaces and of course, the seasons. As this is a basket of garden treasures, then ideally the activity will be offered outdoors.

For children in the early stages of development the main learning focus will be around the senses. How do these natural object look, feel, smell, taste and sound? From a very early age the children will be able to indicate their likes and dislikes. Due to their natural inquisitiveness and desire to touch, this activity will develop hand/eye coordination and upper body muscle development in babies during periods when they are on their stomachs and can practice lifting their upper bodies, reaching and stretching.

As children get older the focus will shift into much wider areas. You can use this activity to encourage development in areas such as:

- Language development – with the describing and naming of the objects that have been collected.

- Mathematical development – encouraging the children to count, match, sort and develop their knowledge.

Time for you to think

- Did you provide enough variety in the collection you created and was there enough space and time to allow the children to really explore?

- Were there any items that the children were keen to collect that were not appropriate? How could you avoid this issue next time?

- Did any children show preferences for particular items? How can you use these further?

- Did all of the items that you/they chose prove appropriate for handing without risk? If not how do you change them or change the way you presented them?

- Do you think you got the balance right between observing and contributing?

- Creative development – allowing the children to create patterns, shapes and pictures with their objects.

Responding to children's and babies' interests

By watching and recording how babies respond to different objects and their likes and dislikes, you can then go on to plan other activities that consolidate learning opportunities.

Listening to children and talking with them

This activity really benefits from long periods of listening to the talk of children whilst they are engaged in their exploration.

With babies and young children you would introduce this type of activity with lots of language.

Babies at the early stages of language development will be engaged by the sound and intonation of your voice as much as they will be by the objects. Your excited and enthusiastic tones will reassure and encourage them.

Always use real names for objects and plenty of descriptive words when talking about them to babies and younger children: "Look at this! A bright green shiny leaf! That feels lovely and smooth!".

Most importantly, remember that is not just what you say but how you say it!

If a child is looking very engrossed in their exploring of objects and is clearly showing a preference for something in particular, it is often better to wait and ask retrospective questions like: "I see you have made a big pile of fir cones. What is it you like about them so much?".

This means you won't break their thought process by asking the same question at the time.

Learning about outdoor art

Young children often find magic in what we would class as the most mundane of things. They also like to scavenge for finds and then use those finds to create pictures, patterns and shapes within their outdoors environment.

In this activity you will encourage the children to look for a variety of different shapes and patterns within the outside environment as well as collect natural objects to create their own. This can be done on an individual small scale or on a large scale with a group.

The shapes and patterns that you will be able to see will change depending on the weather and the seasons. In winter, the trees are bare and their branches make very intricate patterns against the cloudy sky. In summer, leaves hide those branches but the sun shining through those leaves makes a whole new set of light patterns on the ground below.

It is important to get children not only to look at the small things that are easily held in their hands or right in front of their faces, but to draw their attention to the huge magnitude of the world. Try getting them to stand at the bottom of a tree and looking way up into its branches or lying on their back and tracking moving clouds or tiny aeroplanes in the sky.

What do you need to do beforehand?

This is the sort of activity that you could do any time you are outside. It doesn't take much preparation and can be different every time you do it.

Before you go out with the children have a good look at the permanent structures in your immediate environment, things such as buildings with rectangular doors or circular windows, bird houses, bicycles with round wheels. These will provide a good base for your teaching of regular 2D and 3D shapes.

Next have a look at your natural environment. Have you got enough uncultivated space for the children to go and have a good old 'rummage'. Is there a wide selection of objects of various textures for them to collect and use?

You might want to enhance your outdoor space by adding natural objects such as feathers, cobbles, bark, shells, slate etc. for the children to work with.

If children are making their own individual work of art then they often like to have a space that is defined as 'theirs'. If you have paving slabs as part of your outdoors these are perfect. If not, try giving each child a pillow case that they can lay on the floor and use as a makeshift canvas.

An opportunity to learn about outdoor art

There is a lot of opportunity for language development in an activity like this. Not just in respect of identifying and naming the objects that children find and use in their pattern making, but also in describing their texture and scent. Children will also be learning a great deal about the properties of the items that they find. Do they snap/do they crumble/are they hard/are they soft?

Children need time to really explore their finds and also to see what will happen to their creations when they are left out in the elements. Will they dissolve in the rain? Why did the petals blow away in the wind but the stones stay where they put them? To allow children to investigate these answers, their creations need to be left out and not tidied away!

Alongside learning about the irregular patterns of nature, this is also a great opportunity to introduce children to concepts such as regular shape recognition and colour recognition. Remember that although it is true that (most) leaves are green, they are not all the same shade of green and the more vocabulary that we can expose children to, the more chance they have of using it.

Responding to children's and babies' interests

This is a very open-ended activity. Some children will enjoy transporting the various items that they find to various places in the garden and then carefully positioning them there. Having lots of little collections (for toddlers these might only be stones!) dotted all over your outdoor space will make this easier for children to accomplish. Children love to collect and for some, the collecting of all of the precious garden treasure is more of a pleasure than the creation of their pattern or art! Make sure that you always have collection bags, baskets or boxes available for children to use. A stack of plantpots will do just as well and they might get the added surprise of a sleeping woodlouse when they come to use it.

If you are going to make a larger sculpture then bear in mind that it is often difficult for young children to visualise something on a large scale and from an aerial view. Make sure you spend lots of time discussing what the children might like to make. Help the children by talking about colour, pattern and shape using the real thing or photographs to look at.

This activity can run continually all year.

- Was there enough variety of texture and shape in my outdoor environment?

- Did the children have enough space to work in? Were the children able to collect and transport all of the items that they needed?

- Did the children want to pattern-make alone or collaboratively?

- What 'knowledge' differences were there?

Listening to children and talking with them

Young children can see the world in a very different way to adults. We need to make sure that we understand what it is they want to do, so that we can help them achieve it.

If a child is really absorbed in their creation then they are often best left to get on with it. We may feel like we are doing the right thing by intervening or suggesting what they do next but we actually risk stifling opportunities for development and interrupting their deep-level learning.

If a child has had limited experience of textures and is not keen to join in, then they need a much slower introduction to the world of outdoors, maybe starting with a familiar texture and working from there.

If a child has lots of experience, then our role is to extend their use of language and concept of space – so an autumn leaf might be 'auburn' instead of just 'red' and a pattern might become a 3D sculpture rather than just being flat on the ground.

If children are very young or have not been exposed to a wide range of learning experiences, then they may need some support when it comes to choosing what to do. If children are stuck for an idea, talk about lots of options to inspire them, but make sure that you go with their ideas and not yours.

Learning about 'real' experiences from favourite stories

Many of the stories that we read to children have some element of 'growing' in them from the old traditional tales like *Jack and the Beanstalk*, *The Enormous Turnip* and more recent stories like *Pumpkin Soup* by Helen Cooper (Corgi, 1999). Although we read to the children about the planting and harvesting, chopping and mixing, cooking and tasting – many of them will not have had the opportunity to try all of the elements from start to finish. If we want them to truly understand what it feels and smells like to push a seed deep into the

What do you need to do beforehand?

If you are planning this activity well in advance, then make sure that you have checked the sowing and harvesting time for all of the vegetables that you want to use.

Also make sure that you have got enough space – as some pumpkins can grow really big and beans really tall.

Do a bit of research when you are looking at the stories that you might use as your inspiration and check how easy the vegetables are to grow. There is nothing worse than going out to harvest your carrots by pulling up their large leafy tops, only to find a teeny-tiny carrot underneath.

If you can, try and source a number of different versions of the stories that you are going to use. Not only is it interesting to discuss the differences in how the stories are told, but also different styles of illustration can be a great talking point and inspiration for the children's own art.

ground, compare that with what it feels like and smells like to chop it up and then again when you cook it – then we have to let them do it!

As a longer-term project you would ideally plant ahead and ensure that you had fruit and vegetables that you could match to familiar stories, but in the short term, even if the children have not planted and harvested the produce, they can still use it to cook with.

If you want to give children the experience of pulling vegetables up out of the ground to reinforce where they came from, you can buy fresh ones with the leaves still on and plant them in a container or tub for the children to dig up. Don't be tempted to use plastic ones, it really is not the same!

An opportunity to learn about 'real' experiences from favourite stories

This activity gives the children an opportunity to explore 'real' experiences that they see and read about in the pages of their favourite books. It helps to develop their vocabulary and also their understanding of the process of turning real-life events into stories and stories into real-life events.

To really consolidate the children's understanding of the activity you could create a 'parallel' version of the story that you are looking at or create an alternative version that is modelled around the same idea.

For example, the story of *Pumpkin Soup* involves the animals making a special soup. With the help of an adult, the children can also use the vegetables they have grown and harvested to follow the recipe in the book to make and taste some 'pumpkin soup' of their own.

This particular story is also about friendship and sharing – so there are lots of aspects of personal and social skills and feelings that you can discuss as part of the process.

Once the children have made and tasted the soup, do they like it? This is a great chance to explore how children are able to express their personal preferences, likes and dislikes.

Responding to children's and babies' interests

This activity has lots of elements to it, so children's interests could take off in a number of directions.

When you are harvesting your vegetables, children often get carried away with the notion of uprooting things as they are fascinated about what lives under the soil and how roots work. Make sure you plant plenty of extras so that everyone can have a go.

Children may well be inspired by other stories that they know and want to plant or harvest other garden crops so that they can copy that book too.

Root vegetables and their leaves often get nibbled by minibeasts and rodents and this can spark an interest in minibeast and small mammal investigation. So keep a look out for small holes!

Time for you to think

This activity can run continually all year.

- Did the children understand the concept of time and growth? Did they expect to see the fruit and vegetables fully grown by the next day?

- Did you take the opportunity to explain to the children why some plants grow under the ground and the important job that their roots do?

- When you were harvesting your ingredients, did you give the children time to 'notice'; to really look and investigate the plants and soil?

Listening to children and talking with them

Look at *Pumpkin Soup* with the children and get them to tell you what they think is happening in the story.

Spend some time looking at the recipe and instructions on the front page and talking to the children about what we use instructions for and where else you might find them. You can refer back to the instructions for planting the seeds.

If the children are showing a real interest in cooking, then set up opportunities for them to do some cooking role play.

If they are working outside, then they can use kitchen utensils and 'natural' ingredients such as mud, grass, flower heads and leaves. You could set up a 'mud kitchen' which not only impacts on children's imaginary play but all the lifting, pouring and stirring is good for developing their fine and gross motor skills.

Talking about cooking is often a very effective link with children's home environment. Not every child has got garden space to grow their own vegetables, but many will have experienced cooking in some way, shape or form. Get them to talk about their favourite foods and collect recipes from home for you to try in the setting. You could even make your own cookery book!

Learning about growing from a seed

One of the issues with growing anything with young children is that can take a long time and lots of it happens under the ground where they cannot see it. The purpose of this activity is to give the children a very quick and visual example of how a plant grows from seed.

Through activities like this one, we are building a bank of knowledge that children can apply to events that happen later in their development. When they are pulling carrots out of the soil in the autumn this will help them to remember the tiny seed they planted way back in the spring. If they didn't plant the original seed, it will help them to understand what has happened under the ground to turn a seed into that carrot.

This activity is most appropriate for children who have begun to become inquisitive about why things happen and how things are made. The changes in the seed will be visible on a daily basis which helps to maintain interest and engagement.

What do you need to do beforehand?

This activity involves suspending a number of clear plastic bags from a washing line. At the bottom of each bag there is a strip of cotton wool soaked in water and a bean. You start with one bag and add a new bag every other day. Once you have seven bags on your washing line you should be able to see the full life cycle of a bean. The clear plastic bag allows the children to see both roots and shoots.

You must soak a dried bean in water for two days before you put it into your 'bean bag'. Don't forget to keep the cotton wool damp but not wet.

Make sure that you have space for a washing line that gets enough light for the beans to be able to grow.

Give the children lots of experience of handling different varieties of dried bean.

Buy (or grow) real bean pods and let the children open them up to discover the beans for themselves.

Buy a variety of bean and seed products that we can eat (baked beans, bean salad) and let the children taste them so that they appreciate that with lots of plants we eat the seeds as well as the plant.

An opportunity to learn about growing from a seed

Children will be seeing at first hand all of the stages of growth and will have the opportunity to name all of the parts of the plant as they appear. Children could also be given the opportunity to see that if the seed is not watered or given light it will die. Whether or not you add this dimension to the activity will depend on the age and understanding of the children.

Due to the 'staged' nature of the activity they will also be able to compare and contrast the same plant at different stages of its growth. There would be opportunities with this activity to introduce the use of ICT with a digital camera or handheld video. Children could create a picture diary recording how their seeds grew.

With any activity looking at growth there is lots of opportunity to develop children's mathematical awareness and use of mathematical language with phrases like 'taller than' and 'shorter than'. This would also be a good opportunity to use non-standard measure to record growth such as cubes or buttons.

If you use beans for this activity then you can link your work to familiar stories like *Jack and the Beanstalk* and *Jasper's Beanstalk* by Nick Butterworth (Hodder, 2008).

Responding to children's and babies' interests

As children realise what is happening to the bean, it may inspire them to want to try and grow other plants from seed.

Look for seeds in the food that you are eating. Challenge the children to find the seeds in fruit like apples and oranges and in less obvious fruit like bananas and Kiwi. Look at the bits of food that you would normally throw away. Are there any pips or seeds in it?

Citrus fruit pips grow relatively quickly on a warm window sill if they are about an inch deep in compost.

If the children show an interest in growing more seeds, let them tell you what you need to help the seed to grow. It is important that you follow their instructions – especially if they are wrong. If the seed does not grow then there is lots of powerful learning in investigating why.

Add an extra 'bean bag' to your washing line but this time make sure it has water but no light. Add another that has light but dry cotton wool.

Give the children time to think and talk about why the seeds aren't growing rather than you just telling them. You can help to shape their thinking by asking lots of open questions; "I wonder why these ones didn't grow?", "Did they have everything the same as the other beans?".

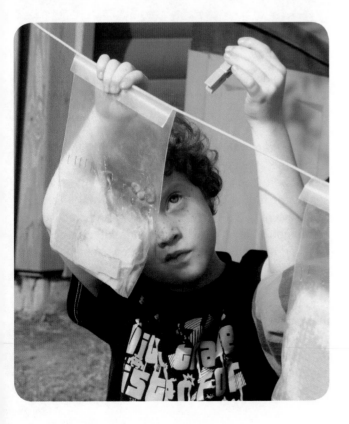

Time for you to think

- Were the children involved enough in the preparation of this activity? Was there enough opportunity for 'hands on' participation?

- Did the beans grow in the bag? If not, why?

- Did I allow the children to look for answers rather than tell them?

- Could I have linked this activity to any other area of learning, including home-setting?

- How can I keep their interest in 'growing'?

Listening to children and talking with them

As children are experiencing anything for the first time they can be prone to misconceptions and getting the process wrong. They are more likely to understand that their seed needs water to grow if they discover it through a real experience rather than just being told it is a fact by an adult.

If during this activity a child tells you something like; "That bean did not grow because it was planted on a Tuesday and beans only grow if they are planted on Thursdays!", then it is important to take their reasoning (days of the week) and use that to help the child disprove their own theory. You could label all of the bags on the days they were planted and then ask the child what they notice.

When they have reached the conclusion that it is not to do with days of the week – don't tell them the answer – let them explore their next theory until they get it. By doing this we are showing the children that their ideas are valued and listened to and we are also teaching them how to think around a problem until you find a solution and not just wait to be told the answer.

If a child plants some cress and sees it grow in two days and thinks if they plant an apple pip in two days they will have a tree, let them try it and then help them to investigate why it didn't work.

Learning about size and scale

As children grow, it is important that they get a concept of their size in relation to the world around them. What are they taller than? What are they smaller than? How do they know if they have grown? This activity provides some great opportunities for children to consider that not all things grow at the same rate or to the same height. A cress seed will grow quickly but not end up being very tall whereas a tree will grow slowly but could

What do you need to do beforehand?

This activity takes a bit of preparation as you have to take a full-length photograph of each child before you start. The photographs work best if they are taken face on. Make sure you get their feet and the top of their head in as this is essential for measuring.

The photographs are going to get some fairly rough treatment in the outdoor environment so make sure you laminate them first.

Ideally you want the 'mini-me's to stand up on their own so that the children can position them easily and move them around. The best thing I have found for this is to stick them to small bottle like the ones you would get a yogurt drink in.

Make sure that when you are thinking about what to plant in your outdoor space that you plant vegetation that will give you some diversity in terms of height, width and shape.

If you are specifically using your 'mini-me's to enhance language development and storytelling then ensure that you have a range of planting that corresponds to stories the children are familiar with and will be able to engage in. Size is crucial to this activity so make sure you have plants that will be both big and small.

end up being huge. As you plant various plants and flowers across the year, the children will get to see and consider this in a number of situations.

The first step in this activity is for the children to create a 'mini-me'. Having themselves in a miniature form is very powerful as they can compare and contrast with something that is extremely familiar. There will be lots of opportunity for the children to learn and practise mathematical language, like 'bigger' and 'biggest', 'smaller' and 'smallest', as well as positional language such as 'in front of' and 'beside'.

When the children are comparing their 'mini-me's and themselves to different plants and flowers in their early stages of growth, it is a good time to ask the children to predict which ones they think will grow the tallest and the smallest, which will grow the fastest and which will grow the slowest. Don't forget that root vegetables grow under the ground. Ask the children how big they think they will grow. Record their answers and then wait and see!

An opportunity to learn about size and scale

Not only will children be getting first-hand experience of size, this activity is also a little bit magical in that allows them to transport themselves into a completely different world where everyday objects now tower above them.

There are lots of opportunities for storytelling and language development as the children take their 'mini-me's on their travels around the environment. What would happen if they really did shrink down to the size of their mini-me? What would the world look like? They can also use their 'mini-me's to put themselves into well-known stories. They could climb a real beanstalk or they could pull up an enormous turnip, their imagination is the only limit. The children need to be given lots of time to explore and also compare and contrast their findings. Are all apples the same size? Why not? Can they find one that is bigger than their mini-me?

Responding to children's and babies' interests

If your main teaching focus is in relation to size, shape and position, encourage the children to use their mini-me in their small-world play.

Time for you to think

- Was there enough variety in the things the children could compare themselves and their mini me to?

- Did I introduce enough elements of challenge for the more able children?

- How could I extend this experience using other familiar stories and rhymes?

- Could I enhance this activity in the future with any small world play opportunities?

- Did the children talk about any interests that I could use to help me plan for them?

- How could I ask the parents to follow up this activity at home?

Not only do you have the added bonus of the language development that this sort of play can bring along with it, but you are more likely to get a higher level of engagement from the children.

This will, in turn, extend the length of the activity – giving you lots more opportunities to teach and assess what they know.

If the children are enjoying measuring with their mini-me then you can extend their learning by using non-standard measures such as counting cubes.

Listening to children and talking with them

As well as the obvious benefits of size and shape work, children will often use their mini-me to express their thoughts and feelings because it is not the 'real' them.

It is important to listen to what they are saying and allow them to change the story to suit their needs rather than encouraging them to stick to the story.

How the children interact with their little figures can also give you a really good indication of their personal preferences, likes, dislikes and interest.

This is important information for you to record, as it will help you shape the activities that you plan for them in the future. The more that you plan your activities around your children's interests, the higher the level of engagement from them will be.

Create play opportunities indoors and out that will allow the children to relive and re-enact events that have taken place in your setting – that they have enjoyed and also may have found difficult. You can recreate a mini-version of your outside play space indoors and let the children explore it all over again.

If there were any activities that they were anxious about or if they displayed any inappropriate behaviour, you can explore these through your miniature play.

Learning about things that are safe to eat in your outdoor space

In this activity the children are going to learn what is safe to touch and eat in your outdoor environment and what they should leave well alone. It important that you train the children to always ask if they are in any doubt about what they are about to pick or eat and never leave a child unsupervised in an area where there might be something that is potentially harmful. It is important that the children have the opportunity to collect the different leaves, fruit and berries themselves, as then they will know exactly where they came from.

What do you need to do beforehand?

Always make sure that you have done your nature research first. Fill in a benefit and risk assessment so that you are clear about any apparent risks. You need to give careful thought to what you are going to say to the children about eating leaves and berries that they find outside. How will you get them to recognise the difference between picking and eating a strawberry, but not a poisonous berry from a tree?

Identify two big spaces in your outdoor areas where the children will have plenty of space to sort out what they have collected. Make sure that your two spaces are clearly identified as 'safe' and 'unsafe'. You might use a picnic rug for one and a skull and crossbones flag for the other.

As the children are going to be doing the collecting, make sure that they have all got a paper bag or basket to put their finds into. If you are going to encourage the children to research using books, make sure you have plenty to go around.

Once the children have emptied out their collection bags then they will work with an adult to sort their finds in to things that taste yummy and things that will give you a sore tummy.

It is a good opportunity to model to the children how you would use books or, for the older children, the Internet to research any plant that you don't know and even make a book of your own.

An opportunity to learn about things that are safe to eat in your outdoor space

Young children are naturally curious and when they are exploring the outdoors will rely heavily on all of their senses. They will use hearing, sight and touch the most, but it is perfectly natural for them to want to smell and taste. As not everything that is growing in your outdoor space is good to eat, it is important that the children have a really good understanding of what is safe.

Not only will they be learning about the vegetation in your outdoor space, but you will also be showing them how we can use symbols as warnings of danger and safety like a skull and crossbones for danger and a smiley face for safe.

The children will also have the opportunity to engage in some early research skills as they use reference books and the Internet to identify unfamiliar plants and flowers. They will also get the opportunity to practise their matching skills as they compare the vegetation they have found to the information they discover.

Once you have identified which of the plants you have are safe to touch and eat, then the children should get the opportunity to do just that. You can introduce the children to new experiences and tastes such as dandelion salad and nettle or mint tea.

Responding to children's and babies' interests

Children are often fascinated by the idea that something can be poisonous or bad for you. Often the younger the child the less inhibited they will be about popping something into their mouth – so you have to be very clear about the potential dangers.

Knowing what is edible in your outdoor space might inspire the children to want to grow more edible plants that can be eaten raw or in cooking. You might want to have a collection of plant and seed catalogues that the children can look through to give them some ideas.

If the children are showing real interest in warning other people about the dangers of eating a poisonous plant then you could encourage them to make posters using pictures or the real thing. Not only do they get to write their own warnings but they can also improve lots of elements of their fine motor dexterity.

It is also worth considering the strong possibility that if you are talking about things being poisonous, the children will quite naturally want to talk about what would happen if you did eat some.

Time for you to think

- Were the children able to access the whole space for their investigation, with enough time?

- Was I clear in my expectations of what I wanted the children to do? How can I develop this?

- Is there anything that I need to put in place immediately as a follow up to this activity?

- Did I have enough resources to allow the children to research the vegetation, including tasting 'safe' food? Did I have a variety of resources, such as photographs and books?

Listening to children and talking with them

Get the children to tell you what they are going to do so that you can be sure that everyone is clear.

You want them to think about and consider how they are going to go about this task. Rather than just give them an instruction you could ask them: "I wonder what would happen if…" or "What could we do when…". By asking them this sort of open question you are asking for a response that requires some thought from them.

You could talk to the children about what they think you should do about any plants growing in your setting that might give them a sore tummy. They might suggest getting rid of them or they might suggest selling them to witches to make magic potions!

By listening to what the children say when they come to empty out their collection bags, you can see which children have a good idea about what is safe and which children have no idea! This will help you to support specific children in your discussions.

Children may have genuine concerns about what might happen to them if they eat a food which is bad for them. You need to be prepared for any questions they may have about being poisoned or dying as these are favourite topics of conversation with lots of young children!

Learning about garden chorus

Listening is a skill that children need to learn and practise over time. The ability to listen well can have a significant impact on children's attainment throughout their educational career. The outdoor environment can provide a wealth of different sounds for children to identify. Some of these sounds will be usual, if created by animals that regularly visit your outdoor space and some will change depending on

What do you need to do beforehand?

Before you take the children outside to listen, it is a really good to have an idea of what they might hear so you can give them specific things to listen out for.

If there is a particular bird song that you often hear, try and find out which bird makes it and have some pictures of it for the children to look at. This way they can develop their looking and listening skills at the same time!

With older children you might want to encourage them to group the sounds that they are hearing into different categories such as 'vehicle sounds' (like cars, trains and aeroplanes), bird song, animal noises and weather.

Don't forget that you can change the way we hear the sounds that the weather makes by listening from different places. The rain will sound different on a glass window, in a tent or under an umbrella. If you want the children to experience this then make sure you have any resources close at hand.

Is it easier to focus on listening if you close your eyes? Why? Ensure that children are steady before they close their eyes.

the weather or the seasons. Whatever the season and whatever the weather, there is always something for children to listen to outdoors.

An opportunity to learn about garden chorus

This activity will provide your children with the opportunity to listen and identify different sounds that they can hear.

It also offers the opportunity for them to then try and identify those sounds and link them to an animal, object or weather type.

To further broaden the impact of this activity you could collect a range of natural objects such as sticks, leaves, stones and bark and encourage the children to explore the sorts of sounds they can create by handling those objects in a variety of different ways. Once the children become familiar with the sort of sounds that they can make, then you can ask them if they can recreate the sounds that they hear using the natural materials they have collected.

Responding to children's and babies' interests

This activity can lead off in all sorts of directions depending on what captures the children's imaginations. If they hear an aeroplane you could talk to them about where they think it might be going, or where they would like to go if they were on it.

You can extend children's thinking by asking open-ended questions or giving them ideas to investigate and problems to solve. If they hear the sound of a car you could ask them if they think that all cars sound the same? How would they find out?

At different times of year, your outdoor space might be visited by different kinds of birds, many who may have travelled from the other side of the world. This is a great opportunity to talk to the children about their immediate locality and the wider world outside.

One of the most common things to hear in your outdoor space is a 'rustle' made by an animal often in the bushes or trees. This is a great opportunity to develop children's imaginations and creative vocabulary when you talk to them about what it could be and what it might look like.

Time for you to think

Before you do this activity again:

- Did you have enough knowledge about the sorts of sounds you were likely to hear?

- Did you collect other resources that would have supported children's listening skills like books and photographs?

- Could you create opportunities to change the weather sounds that children hear by using resources like umbrellas or tents?

- Could you add other tuned and percussion instruments to the natural ones you made or collected to help the children to replicate the sounds they heard? Try things like small drums, maracas or a rain maker.

It may be useful, particularly with babies who are not yet mobile, to physically take them to different areas of your outdoor space so that you can ensure that they are nearer a particular sound and can therefore focus their attention on it.

As the children get older it can be a useful exercise to get them to be very still and listen to what they can hear. It might even be useful to create a 'sound lotto' card where they can mark off familiar sounds when they hear them.

Listening to children and talking with them

Some children will not have a wide-ranging experience of the outside world and may have no idea what they are hearing even if it is a really familiar sound to some of their peers. These children will need lots of repetition of this type of activity – with a focus on the sounds that it is easy for them to attribute to something that they know well, such as traffic.

The process of being able to pick out a particular sound, hear it and then experiment with other resources to try and replicate it is a much more complex process and you should work towards

it with children who have had lots of experience of listening to a wide variety of sounds.

Often, when listening to a sound without being able to see what it has made it, children will give you an answer that is very different from the actual answer, or the one that you expected. This is a great opportunity to explore your children's thinking further to find out what they think made that noise and how. Sometimes this situation can be used as an important opportunity to correct misconceptions and sometimes it can be used as a brilliant opening to imaginative play and language development. If a child is really unsure about what they have heard, instead of just telling them the answer you could give them a series of clues to help them to solve the mystery and find out for themselves.

Learning about seasonal scent

As the title suggests, this is an activity that really engages children's sense of smell. As the seasons change, so does the scent of your outdoor space. Scent doesn't only come from sniffing flowers, but also from leaves, seeds, bark and a host of other garden features. The children will be using many of their other senses when they are looking for, handing and collecting their scent-filled treasures. We should encourage the children to look beyond the obvious and try smelling other things like different types of soil and roots.

Don't forget that the smell doesn't always have to be nice and sweet. We want children to experience as wide a range as possible.

What do you need to do beforehand?

Before the children get the opportunity to make their own 'seasonal scent' take them into different areas of your outdoor space and let them be 'sniffing detectives'. First of all, can they identify any sort of smell? Then, can they locate where it is coming from?

Once they have had a good sniff of the outdoor space then you can get them to collect anything that they think they would like to mix together to make their seasonal scent.

As you are going to be asking the children to collect items from around your outdoor space make sure that you have provided something for them to put their finds in.

When they have their collections you are going to encourage them to experiment with crushing them up together and mixing them with water to release their fragrance. The larger the variety of pots, jars and stirring implements you can provide, the better. A pestle and mortar is best for crushing and jars and bottles with lids are good for shaking.

It is also worth remembering some sticky labels so that you can identify who the scent belongs to and remember what is in it!

An opportunity to learn about seasonal scent

This activity will provide your children with the opportunity to learn about how to identify different smells in the outdoors and also how to release the smell from some objects using techniques like crushing or adding water. Many children really enjoy the experimental aspect of this sort of activity.

You can make strong links to other aspects of learning such as communication, language and literacy through the use of stories and rhymes about spells and potions. Children will also have opportunities to develop their mathematical knowledge as well as their knowledge and understanding of how different things look, feel and smell.

Allow the children to enjoy smelling what they make but be sure to remind them not to eat the mixtures that they are creating. This activity should always be done under the careful supervision of an adult.

Responding to children's and babies' interests

Some children like to stick with the sweet smells of flowers and are also attracted by the colours of their petals. Encourage these children to tear the petals apart with their fingers as well as crushing them or chopping with scissors. This sort of interest can provide great opportunities to encourage children to make and bottle their own petal perfume. You could even set up a 'pretend' petal perfume shop outdoors and design labels for your product. Decide on a price and then get the children to use real or pretend pennies to sell it.

If you have herbs in your outdoor area then there is the potential to use this activity to introduce the children to some familiar scents and some that might be new to them. You can then go on to use the flavours you have discovered to cook with. Mixing fresh herbs into play dough allows the children to carry on experiencing their scent in a different way.

Lost of children enjoy the sensation of using the pestle and mortar to crush up the various unusual items that they have found. Often they will link this experience to the making of spells or potions. This can really fire their imaginations and lead to some fantastic storytelling – as long as they don't attempt to eat or drink their potion. Although you want to encourage their imaginary play, it would be worth reminding them that their potion making is just pretend.

If you would ilke to extend this play even further you could get the children to build an outdoor shop using plant pots, pieces of wood, stones etc. The shop could sell their perfumes and potions.

Depending on the age of the children you are working with, you could enhance your shop with price stickers, number recognition, real money, counting... the list is endless.

Time for you to think

Before you do this activity again:

- Did the children try a variety of items to crush and smell? If there are no flowers when you next do this activity, what will you use?

- Did you have enough time afterwards to reflect on what the children had found out? Did you use that information in your planning afterwards?

- Have you checked that no new plants have grown that might pose a danger?

Listening to children and talking with them

For very young children or children who may have had limited first-hand experience, start with very familiar smells like grass or fruit. Depending on the needs and development of the children you are working with, the outcomes you would expect from this activity might be very different. Some children may struggle to find the vocabulary they need to describe what they smell, whereas others will have a range of words to use.

Be flexible in your approach and remember what the underlying outcome of the activity was. If you liked the idea of making petal perfume and then the children decide that they want to make dandelion soup, then go with their interest and engagement.

Using smells is a good way to get children to express their likes and dislikes. This activity is also an opportunity to extend their use of language by asking them to explain why they do or don't like a smell. Smell is one of the senses that works very effectively as a 'memory jogger'. This activity often leads to children recounting experiences that included the same or similar smell. It is important to take time to listen to the children, share in their story and ask them questions about what they are saying. This helps them to focus and think about a response to your question. It also lets them know that you are interested in what they are talking about.

Learning about texture trail

In this activity you want the children to find as many different textures in your outdoor space as possible. Depending on the age of the children, this activity will have a different focus. If the children you are working with are very young or have not had a great deal of first-hand experience of different textures, then the activity will be very much led by the adult and you will be introducing the children to an ever widening variety

What do you need to do beforehand?

It is essential that you know your outdoor place and are aware of what the children are likely to find when they are out there.

If you are going to ask the children to match an object to your describing word, then make sure that they have a firm understanding of what the word means.

Very young children need lots of experience of using a word in the correct context before they can begin to use it independently. A toddler might not understand the word 'rough', but they may understand the term 'bumpy'. All children develop language at different rates so you would need to match the words that you use to each child's stage of development and not just their age.

If the children are going to create a map for their texture trail, then decide if they are going to do this individually. If together, you will create a plan of your outdoor space and then the children will stick onto the plan what they found and where.

Make sure that you have a wide range of textures for the children to select and experience. Spread them out around your space so that they don't find them all at once.

of touch experiences and also vocabulary to describe what they are feeling.

Bear in mind how children of different ages might need more or less support in accessing this activity. Babies will be limited in their ability to get mobile and collect items and although many young children have tonnes of enthusiasm, they don't always have a well-developed sense of danger.

If the children are older and/or more experienced, then the challenge for them is to show what they know and find as many different textures as they possibly can. Can they find something soft/hard/rough/smooth/wet/dry? And so on.

The children are likely to be handling materials that could be rough or spikey, so make sure that you have completed your benefit and risk assessment and removed anything that might be a real hazard.

An opportunity to learn about texture trail

Texture is something that you can feel, but you can also see it and use language to describe it, so this activity can potentially offer a number of diverse opportunities. It is also an activity that you can do at different times of the year, achieving some very different results. Encourage the children to search outside of their immediate eye level and arm reach. Suggest that they look 'up high', 'down low', 'in and out' and 'side to side'. Be clear with the children whether they are allowed to pick and collect the items or just identify them.

As an alternative you could lead the activity by asking the children to find you something 'soft', 'rough', 'spikey' etc. and then compare and contrast the items that they find. This way the children will have matched a description to an item. You could then use the items they had collected and ask them to give you the word to describe their texture.

Responding to children's and babies' interests

Often, children who have not yet had opportunities to experience a wide range of texture can be quite reluctant to touch and feel. This is perfectly normal and the worst thing we can do is to pressure them into it. If this is the case, then start slowly and build up the experiences gradually. Allow these children to watch

Time for you to think

Before you do this activity again:

- Was there a wide-enough range of texture outdoors?

- Were there any textures that the children missed?

- Have I planned any follow-on activities to consolidate this learning?

- Do I need to promote or restrict any area of my outdoor space to provide more opportunity?

- Can I make links between texture outdoors and texture indoors?

- Can I extend this activity by asking the children to hunt for different textures at home?

the other children enjoying the process of touching and talking and let them try in their own time. Most children do eventually!

Any sort of activity that involves a map or a trail often sparks a 'pirate' or explorer interest in children. If this is the case then go with it! It is worth considering what your original learning intention was for the activity and rather than having your pirates find a hoard of chocolate biscuits for their booty, let them find some natural garden treasures.

Listening to children and talking with them

Children learn most effectively in a new experience when they can make lots of connections to past experiences. When we are helping them to try and make sense of what they are learning about, it is really useful to make connections to experiences they have already had. If we are saying that a leaf is 'smooth', to give that statement context and meaning; it is really effective to ask children if they can name something else that is 'smooth' even if it is not exactly the same. Making these sorts of connections in a child's brain is what helps new learning to stick.

The greater the variety and frequency of opportunities a child gets to practise the thing that they have just learned, the more time their brain has to use their new knowledge. Like everything else, the more practice you have at something, the better you get at doing it and that is the just same for your brain.

Once the children have collected lots of different textures and are aware of where they found them in the outdoor space, you can bring these objects indoors and create texture bags or baskets, so that the children can revisit the familiar experience even if they are not outside.

Children will then also have the opportunity to look for matching textures in the indoor environment.

Learning about dandelion magic

This activity is a good one to engage children's interest in the more unusual properties of everyday garden plants and flowers. As we all know, many of our everyday outdoor plants have been used for hundreds of years as medical treatments. Some of you may be aware of the use of a dock leaf to relieve a nettle sting. Very young children can easily be taught to recognise a dock leaf and be shown how to use it in a 'nettle sting emergency'. Even if they don't understand the exact science behind how it works, this is their first experience of the knowledge and understanding of the world that will eventually become chemistry.

Children are always fascinated by garden magic and often by spies and secret agents. This activity is a great combination of the two.

What do you need to do beforehand?

It may sound obvious but make sure that there are plenty of dandelions in bloom before you do this activity. Late spring and early summer is the best time. If the children are picking their own then encourage them to have as long a stem on their dandelion as they can manage – as the longer the stem the more sap they have to draw with.

Although dandelions are not poisonous (and their leaves can be eaten in salad!) their sap is bitter and sticky and not very pleasant when all over your hands, especially if you try to lick it off! Encourage the children to clean their hands as they go and not to put their fingers in their mouth.

This is a great activity to do if you go on a trip to a local field or park. Just remember to take some paper for drawing on and plenty of wipes!

If it is not a sunny day then you will need to bring your dandelion pictures home and warm them up for their magic to work.

The children might show a real interest in their secret mark making and want to take it indoors. Make sure that you have got something to carry your dandelions in to avoid getting their sap all over you and the children.

An opportunity to learn about dandelion magic

'Garden secret agent' is not only an opportunity to learn some early science, it is also a very effective way to engage children in some mark making.

Dandelions have long been associated with the playground rumour that they make you wet the bed. Although picking a dandelion alone will not make you wet the bed there is some truth in the old wives tale. Dandelions are a diuretic and if you ate lots of them then they would cause your body to produce more urine which could in theory make you more likely to wet the bed!

Thankfully we are not going to be eating them, we are going to be mark making with them. If you cut a dandelion off at the stem and then draw with it on white paper, your drawing will be invisible. If you then leave it to dry in the sun or on a radiator the heat will turn the sap brown and your picture will miraculously appear!

This means that if you need to send any secret agent invisible messages you could do it with nothing more than a common or garden dandelion!

Responding to children's and babies' interests

Children are usually fascinated by this process and keen to try it again and again. If the children do show a high level of interest then encourage them to do the same thing with other plants and leaves and see if they get the same result. Be really clear with them what it is acceptable to pick and what they need to leave alone.

Once children have created their secret picture then they can use other natural materials to further enhance it:

- By rubbing a bunch of grass on their paper they will get a green stain;

- Petals of certain flowers will also produce quite a vivid colour when rubbed on white paper.

Dandelion is not the only plant that produces invisible ink, you can also get the same effect by using lemon juice. As I imagine not may of us have lemon trees in our outdoor space, this might be a good way of extending this activity with an indoor focus.

Talk to the children about dandelion clocks and how people believed that they could tell the time and grant wishes. Ask the children why they think they are called dandelions. It is not because they look like a lions mane, but because their leaves are shaped like lions teeth and in French that is 'dent' (meaning tooth) 'de lion' (of the lion) hence dandelion!

The whole idea of being a secret agent could spark a link to all sorts of interest both indoors and out.

Before you do this activity again:

- What questions did the children ask about this activity?

- How could I have taken it forward?

- Did I have enough resources?

- How could I plan to link this activity to other areas of learning?

- Did this activity capture all children's interests?

Listening to children and talking with them

Because of its simplicity and the availability of dandelions during the summer months, this is a great activity to suggest to children that they do to 'trick' an adult at home.

Ask the children to bring in any dandelion magic work that they have done at home so that you can share it. It is a great way of making learning links between your setting and home.

Children might well ask you why the sap goes brown and although you don't want to completely confuse them with a scientific explanation, make sure you have an answer ready at a level they will understand.

It is all to do with carbon compounds and heat! I always explain it like bread going brown in the toaster. The heat dries out the sap just like it dries out the bread and that makes it go brown.

If the children are showing an interest in dandelions then there are other things for them to think about. The dandelion flower will close every evening when it gets dark and open again in the morning when it is light. You may have to take a photo or video this if your children are in bed before it is dark. When the petals are gone they are replaced by tiny 'parachutes'. What are they for? How do they work? How can we find out?

Learning about things trapped in ice

Ice has a great fascination for children of all ages. There is something quite magical about seeing any object suspended in it. The fact that flowers, petals, seeds and twigs are frozen and still, allows children to take their time when looking and examining what they see.

You also have the added bonus of the sensation of the melting ice and the feeling of cold against the skin.

What do you need to do beforehand?

Decide on the size and shape of your ice creation and find appropriate containers. If you are going to hang it up, then make sure you put some string or wool into the water before you put it in the freezer.

When doing this activity with babies and very young children you would create it in advance and the main learning outcomes would be to do with feel, texture and scent.

With older children, part of the learning process is the collecting of items that they would like to freeze and then being involved in the whole process so that they can witness the change of materials from water to ice and eventually back to water again.

Make sure you build in enough time for your creations to freeze thoroughly. I would put them in the freezer for a minimum of four hours, but overnight would make absolutely sure. If you are doing this activity in the winter and the temperature is below freezing then you won't even need to use the fridge, you can just leave your creation out overnight.

There are also opportunities to encourage the children to use other equipment such as magnifying glasses when they are investigating.

You can also add scent and flavouring to the water before you freeze it so that as the ice warms under the children's touch it also releases a fragrance.

This activity is a great one to do with babies and very young children as it has so many possible outcomes.

An opportunity to learn about things trapped in ice

Not only will the children be having a first-hand experience of handling ice but they will also be able to look at other garden treasures in a very unique way. Not only does the ice keep the natural objects very still but it can also act like a magnifying glass and create some interesting visual images. If you make ice 'pictures' that you can suspend in the sunlight then you get the added effect of the light making items like leaves and petals translucent; allowing children to see features like patterns and veins. This is not just an activity for winter. It is one that is equally effective all year round. There is no end to the things that you can freeze in ice. Be warned, once you have tried it, it can become addictive!

Responding to children's and babies' interests

If children have never done this sort of activity before then they are often not sure what to expect. They may well ask questions like "Are the flowers still alive?" and "Will they stay like that for ever?". Depending on the age and experience of the children this sort of questioning is a good opportunity to encourage them to wait and find out the answers for themselves, rather than just tell them.

Sometimes you will find that you have managed to freeze the odd 'creature' that was living on one of the items you put into your creation. Although very unfortunate for the poor creature this does often spark a great deal of interest and fascination. Children have asked me in the past if they can then go on to freeze other live creatures like snails, slugs and bees!

Although for some children this would give a high level of engagement, by knowingly freezing a live creature you are deliberately killing it. If you allow the children to do that then you are clearly giving them the message that killing creatures is an acceptable thing to do. Although for some adults killing a fly would not be the same as killing a bird or a cat, that is their own

Time for you to think

Before you do this activity again:

- Did you have enough containers and were they big enough to hold the items the children selected?

- Did the children understand that the water had turned into ice? How do you know?

- Were you able to provide a range of items for the children to freeze? What could you add for next time?

- Now that the children have had the experience of making ice creations could you expand the outcomes of the activity by putting their creations in various places in your outdoor area and see which melt first? Why might that be?

personal view. Young children do not have the same complex methods of reasoning as adults, so for them; killing is killing.

Make sure you have prepared your answer in advance or you will end up with a lot of minibeast casualties on your hands!

Using magnifying glasses to really examine the contents of your ice creation will often reveal a tiny hidden treasure like a minibeast or a seed.

Listening to children and talking with them

Make sure that you can identify all of the items from your outdoor space that children want to put into the freezer. If there is something you are not sure about then use the opportunity to look it up together.

Ask the children why they have made the choices they have made and what they think will happen once the creation goes into the freezer.

If the children choose to freeze berries or flower heads these will often float on the top of the water – much to the frustration of the children. This is a

great opportunity to discuss with them why this might be and what you could do to stop it from happening.

When your creations come out of the freezer it is interesting to find out what the children think will happen to them now. Will they stay like ice for ever? How could we stop them from melting? When the weather gets cold enough they won't even have to use the freezer, they will be able to make their creations outdoors.

In the summer, your ice creations will usually melt within an hour; in the winter they will hang in the trees for days without melting. It is good to do this activity several times across the year and compare and contrast results with the children.

Learning about sprouting socks

This activity is all about seeds: why plants have them and how they grow. If the children haven't got a great deal of knowledge about different types of seeds or where seeds come from, then you would need to show them lots of different shapes, colours and sizes. Ideally you would collect these from your own outdoor space wherever you could, but if that proves difficult, then there are lots of packet seeds on the market which you could go and buy with the children from the supermarket or garden centre.

What do you need to do beforehand?

Check your outside space for any potential hazards for children who will be walking in their socks.

The more places that they can go, the more chance they have got of picking up a variety of seeds.

Make sure you have got enough pots and compost for everyone's socks.

If your outdoor area has not got any/many planted areas you can still do this activity but you would have to populate the space with a variety of seeds like cress and grass before the children go for their 'sock walkabout'.

Prepare lots of open questions to prompt the children with during the activity – to really get them thinking about what they are doing and what might happen.

If you are using different coloured socks, ask the children if they think the colour of the sock will make a difference.

Decide whether you are going to use this as a knowledge of the world activity about seed growth or an activity to build imagination about a magical sock plant!

An opportunity to learn about sprouting socks

Through the process of this activity we want the children to get a basic understanding of why a plant produces a seed and what that seed then needs to enable it to grow into a new plant. The children will also be able to see from the activity that even though plants do not freely move around, their seeds do. Not only are seeds made to be mobile, they are moved around in a variety of ways. Encourage the children to look at how many different plants and flowers that you have got in your outdoor space. Even in the smallest of outdoor spaces there will be lots (especially if you include grass!).

Then ask the children to imagine how many seeds there must be in and around each plant. Some are so small that they are difficult for us to see and some so big that it is hard to miss them.

Next tell the children that they are going to collect some seeds and add a challenge: not with their hands, but with their feet!

Give each child a pair of white socks and get them to walk all around your outdoor space including any overgrown bits. If you haven't got white socks then you can use another colour but the beauty of the white sock is that it makes it much easier to see the dirt and anything else that is picked up off the ground.

When their socks are nice and dirty, take them off, put them in a plant pot which is about half full of compost, cover the socks with more compost and water well. Then you need to put your pot on a warm windowsill.

The children are often bemused by the fact that you have just buried and watered their socks. This is a good opportunity for you to assess their understanding and encourage their thinking processes. Ask them what they think is going to happen. Don't tell them the answer even if they get it right. Tell them they will have to wait and see. Keep watering and very soon shoots should start sprouting.

Responding to children's and babies' interests

Children are often convinced that nothing will happen because you can't grow socks! Sometimes they will ask if it is a sock tree that is growing in the pot. The purpose of the activity is not only to help children to understand what plants need to help them to grow, but also to help them to understand how plants can appear in different places without legs of their own.

You might want to plant a pair of socks that has been worn in an area with lots of plants and vegetation and also a pair that have been worn where there is none. Get the children to predict what will happen and say why.

If the children decide that there is a magic sock tree growing in their pot, you might take the decision to go with them on that idea and capitalise on all of the opportunities for creativity and imagination that that scenario offers. But at some point (when no socks appear) you would need to come clean and get the children to investigate another solution as to why things grew when they planted socks.

Time for you to think

- Did you know enough about seeds beforehand?

- Did the children have enough first-hand knowledge about a seed to enable the activity to make sense?

- Were there enough spaces outdoors where seeds could be picked up?

- Did the children make the distinction between how the seeds got in the pot and what they needed to grow? Was your explanation clear or do the children think the plants grew from socks?

Listening to children and talking with them

How plants ensure their survival – by trying to spread their seeds far and wide – can be quite a hard concept for children to understand, as they wouldn't have had to think about this before. To make the thinking process easier for them, relate it to things that they will know and understand, like a dandelion clock and how that is designed to carry seeds on the wind.

You can also show them things like wild bird food that contains seeds and talk about how the bird can carry a seed around in its stomach for miles and then poo it out somewhere completely different. (This is usually a very popular topic of conversation with the boys!)

This is a good opportunity to make sure that your own knowledge is sufficient enough to answer any unexpected questions. If you don't know the answer, turn how you will find out together into a learning experience. Don't just make it up!

Make sure that the children understand how the seed got into the pot (on the sock) but also what that seed then needed to help it to grow.

You could always put a pot of socks in the dark and fail to water another to help children make the learning connections.

Reflections on learning about gardening and growing

No matter how big or small your outdoor space is, hopefully the activities in this book have given you some ideas about how you can use it to interest and inspire your children, as well as take their learning forward.

Hopefully you will now think about that space outdoors as providing all-year-round opportunities to allow you to teach children not only what they need to learn, but also what they want to learn.

As we all know, children are naturally inquisitive and the outdoors gives them plenty of opportunities to explore and find out.

These activities have shown that often your garden can provide spontaneous unplanned opportunities that relate to animal life and weather. You can also plan in advance for things that you know will happen – like rainy days, windy days, hot days and cold days!

Your planning for your outdoor space and planting could also include links to other aspects of learning – like stories, songs and rhymes at different times of the year.

I hope this book helps you to think of your outdoor space as an extension of your everyday learning environment and not just somewhere that you use on sunny days.

Finding out more

- Ofsted (2010) Requirements for risk assessments: www.ofsted.gov.uk/resources/factsheet-childcare-requirements-for-risk-assessment

- Bilton, H. (2010) *Outdoor Learning in the Early Years: Management and Innovation*, Routledge.

- Garrick, R. (2009) *Playing Outdoors in the Early Years*, Continuum.

- Green, A. (2005) *Gardening,* Everything Early Years.

- Hughes, A M. (2010) *Developing Play for the Under 3s*, Routledge.

- Knight, S. (2011) *Risk and Adventure in Early Learning Outdoor Play*, Sage.

- Shilling, R. (2009) Land Art, Cherry Leaf, Land art for kids: www.landartforkids.com

- Ward, S. (2010) *The Early Years Gardening Handbook*, Practical Pre-School Books.

- White, J. (2011) *Outdoor Provision in the Early Years*, Sage.

England: Statutory Framework for the Early Years Foudation Stage (2012): www.foundationyears.org.uk/early-years-foundation-stage-2012/

Northern Ireland: CCEA (2011) 'Curricular Guidance for Pre-school Education': www.rewardinglearning.org.uk/curriculum/pre_school/index.asp; CCEA (2006) 'Understanding the Foundation Stage': www.nicurriculum.org.uk/docs/foundation_stage/UF_web.pdf

Scotland: Learning and Teaching Scotland (2010) 'Pre-birth to Three: Positive Outcomes for Scotland's Children and Families': www.ltscotland.org.uk/earlyyears/; The Scottish Government (2008) 'Curriculum for Excellence: Building the Curriculum 3: A Framework for Learning and Teaching'.

Wales: Welsh Assembly (2008) 'Framework for Children's Learning for 3 to 7-year-olds in Wales': http://wales.gov.uk/topics/educationandskills/schoolshome/curriculuminwales/arevisedcurriculumforwales/foundationphase/?lang=en